THE TREE FOR FREE
Copyright © 2013 by Astrid Wenigerova-Noga

All rights reserved. Neither this publication nor any part of this publication may be reproduced or transmitted in any form or by any means, electronic or mechanical, including photocopying, recording or any information storage and retrieval system, without permission in writing from the author.

ISBN: 978-1-77069-787-4

Word Alive Press
131 Cordite Road, Winnipeg, MB R3W 1S1
www.wordalivepress.ca

Cataloguing in Publication information may be obtained from Library and Archives Canada.

Dear Kinlee: You were such a good teamplayer! I am sure the real Pauline Johnson would love to see you impersonating her. In your life, remember the Rutabaga story. It teaches us courage, hard work, discipline, love for others, faith in god And tell about it one day to your children.

Love Astrid WR

Dedicated to our son, Dr. T. I. Noga,
and his children, his "Chinese-Czeckers."

Table of Contents

Introduction

THE MYSTERY OF GOD'S SON'S HUMAN BIRTH ENVELOPES EVERY Christmas in eternal beauty and power. Because the birth was real and also supernatural, it will echo in the universe forever.

You remember many of your Christmases past. Some for you, as for me, became stepping stones on your spiritual pilgrimage. The stories in this, my book of Christmas memories, are true. All of them. Some of my stories might be similar to yours in their spiritual content, so I believe you will like them.

Some Christmas stories are read and reread every year around Christmas: *The Christmas Carol, Charlie Brown's Christmas, The Grinch Who Stole Christmas*, and many others. Some might seem like children's books, and yet they are so much for us adults.

No matter how many times you've read the Bible story of Christ's birth, no matter how many Christmas concerts at your church you've attended, again and again the mystery of God's

Son's human birth will capture you with its eternal beauty and power.

May all your Christmases be bright and white!

—The Author

The Tree for Free

It was a very cold winter Sunday in Grande Prairie, Alberta, four days before Christmas. An old lady and her husband had just stepped out of their daughter's house and closed the door. The woman was clasping under her arm a carton with bold letters, "Free for taking," and a golden sash. With her other hand she grabbed the trunk of a beautiful spruce tree lying in front of the door and asked her husband to help her load it in the back of their white car.

"No way," he replied. "I've cleaned the car for Christmas. I will not let you mess it up with needles, sap and broken branches. You want to do something with the tree, do it yourself."

His words hurt, but she knew her husband well after forty-six years of marriage and knew better than to object or get mad. The woman grabbed the tree and started to pull it past their well-cleaned car, past the neighbouring decorated yard, quietly resolving anew to make somebody happy with this tree.

It was cold, as I've said, and her fur coat reached only to her knees. Her winter boots had high heels, and the tree was much heavier than she expected. By the third house she knew it would take her at least twenty-five minutes of pulling and freezing before she could reach the tree's destination.

As she was passing by a big white and silvery pickup in front of the third house, a man walked out swiftly from the house and called to her, "Hey, madam, do you need help with this tree?"

"Oh, the Lord is good to me!" exclaimed the woman. "You would be willing to help me? Wow! Thank you, thank you!"

The man opened the back of his cleanly swept white and silvery truck and with ease loaded the tree. "So where are we going?" he asked with joy in his voice. "Jump in, madam."

"Just up the road to the pink school," replied the woman with the warmth of thankfulness in her voice. "My daughter paid fifty bucks for the tree but after decorating it with the children found out she and her son are very allergic to its beautiful scent. So they bought a different one and told me this one would get shredded after the season. Not only do I hate fifty bucks going through the shredder, but when we came as refugees to Canada many years ago we had no money for Christmas trees. I remember that time very well. So I would just like to stand the tree by the school and the bus stop up the street. There must be somebody in Grande Prairie who could use a beautiful, expensive Christmas tree for free."

The man looked at the woman, and something from his eyes jumped into hers, a little spark, resembling, perhaps, a little Christmas star. "I grew up in Hythe," he said, "and as children, we would always go to pick up a tree in the forest. Fresh-smelling green trees picked up on fresh-smelling blue days." He added, "My wife prefers clean, not messy, trees," and started the motor.

At that very moment the woman's husband stopped his white car by the truck, knocked on the window and asked the woman where she was going. "Just to the pink school," she replied, deeply embarrassed. The kind truck driver for sure had to realize instantly that this was her husband and that he was unwilling to help her himself. But she had no courage to explain anything, or to joke about it, because that would put her man in a bad light, and after all, he was a good man.

For a short time she didn't know what to say. Finally, she recovered joy in her heart and thanked the man again for helping her. She again expressed her wish that some poor people might notice the tree by the bus stop so she would like to place it there.

"And so we shall!" exclaimed the driver, also with joy.

When they arrived, he stopped the truck, jumped out and pulled the tree out so fast that she, moving slowly on her high heels, could not even help him. He tied it with the golden sash to the signpost, and the woman had nothing to do but to place on the tree's lower branches the carton with the big letters "Free for taking."

The driver wished her Merry Christmas, she wished it back to him, and he jumped in the driver's seat and disappeared.

The woman was very happy. "The Lord is very good to me," she told her husband, who had arrived and was waiting for her. "This help from out of nowhere must be a sign that He really has somebody who needs that tree and who will be thrilled with it. Maybe it's a single mother, maybe a father of several children who hasn't had time to go to the bush to cut a tree. I wonder who it may be! I guess I will never know, but I'm sure the tree will be a source of joy and, I hope, even of thanks to God for His provision."

It was a cold day, as I said, and the car was not warm yet,

but the woman's heart felt warm, and consequently her body did too, in spite of her fur coat reaching just to her knees.

Her husband did not reply, and she was not surprised, because his mind most of the time was dwelling on greater things of this world, such as wars, injustices, political imbalance and the evil descending lately on our planet.

The car was getting warmer. The streets of Grande Prairie disappeared behind them, and the woman watched the white fields with dry grass poking out of the snow along the fences. Occasionally small spruce grew too close to the fence on the ditch side to be cut by the highway service mowers and also out of the reach of the farmers' machinery. Most of them were rather crooked, bent by the winds because they were deprived of the protection offered to little trees in a forest by older, larger companions.

The First Christmas Tree

PERHAPS IT WAS THE DEFORMITY OF THE LITTLE TREES IN the ditch that brought back the memory of a different Christmas tree, the very first Christmas tree that she was able to remember.

In the winter of 1945, she had been a child living in postwar Czechoslovakia. She remembered the ruins in the streets, the sad and angry adults. It was four days before Christmas, and her half-sister, Dana, was packing rationed sugar cubes in paper to become the highly desired part of the Christmas tree's decorations.

Their home industrial city, Ostrava, was burdened with several thousand German prisoners of war. They had to clear ruins, shovel Ostrava's black coal onto wagons, repair roads and railways. Only on Saturday afternoons were some of them permitted to go free for walks. People hated them, so it was never a pleasant outing, but freedom is such a precious thing that they would risk the spitting and cursing.

7

The woman remembered the day when she was a little girl playing in the corridor of their house and one of them, a child soldier, entered and addressed her. He was perhaps sixteen years old. Taken by his blond handsomeness, she fell in love for the first time in her life, but she did not understand her prince.

The woman chuckled at the meager memory of the thin face.

She remembered calling her mom and her mom calling her dad, because he spoke German.

Hans was offering (though forbidden to do so) to work for a few hours in exchange for some food. He was very thin. Dad agreed.

The girl silently watched Hans assess a crooked tree her dad handed him, cut off some lower branches and implant them in the empty spaces of the tree trunk, secure the tree in the stand and present it to her mom with hope and sadness in his eyes. The little girl followed him as he brought the week's supply of coal from the dark, scary cellar. She watched him shoveling snow and finally gulping up the watery soup and dry rye bread. After that she silently watched her dad lay on the table some money and a brown bag with apples and nuts from their own trees, plus a small pack with a picture of a camel on it.

The boy's eyes exploded with joy! He almost laughed; he almost giggled with delight. The little girl knew what it was—a pack of smelly, yucky cigarettes (for sure gotten on the black market). Dad asked him something. The boy answered, "Nein." The little girl understood that word. It meant "no." She guessed Dad asked him if he smoked.

"Aber meine Kamaraden," he continued with an anxious voice. The girl understood that, too. It meant, "But my friends do." The Czech words were very similar to those of the boy.

The woman remembered very clearly how her dad's eyes got wet as he pushed the pack, the money and the bag forward. She knew her dad invited the boy to come back whenever he would be able to.

Now she knew how scarce cigarettes were in those days and how scarce kindness was in those days too.

She never forgot that Christmas tree.

Next morning the tree, looking much better after Hans worked on it, was decorated with real candles, real nuts, packed sugar cubes and, of course, glittery glass balls. It was the most beautiful thing the girl had ever beheld.

In the evening, after a special supper of fried carp and potato salad, Christmas bread and a poppy seed cake, all the children were called to their grandma's apartment, because on Christmas Eve Little Baby Jesus or His angels would visit good children and leave gifts under the Christmas trees. The heavenly beings did not want to be seen.

She and her siblings were told to be absolutely silent and listen for a bell sound, because angels carry Christmas bells with them and upon leaving the house they ring them.

The woman remembered the weak, clear ringing and how quickly, but silently, they all ran back to the tree.

Oh, what a sight! The tree was illuminated with tiny candles and multiple burning sparklers, hissing and sending sparks into the darkness of the room. Near the treetop a paper golden pig was attached, a pig that her father had been given when he was five years old by his mom and his dad, who died just a year later at Christmas. The little girl's heart was bursting with celebration.

After the sparklers fell silent and dark, Dad put on the ceiling's electric lights, and Mom started to pass out gifts provided by the Little Baby Jesus. There were three balls covered by dark blue velvet, so soft, so elegant. There were two dolls for the two girls, not wooden or rag dolls but truly beautiful manufactured toys. Their five-month-old brother got a rocking horse with a mane and tail, and since he was not yet able to rock on it, both girls had a great time with the horsey. There were, of course, practical gifts: hats and mittens knitted from reused wool, and a pair of new shoes for Dad. She could not recollect now what her adult half-sister got from the Baby Jesus.

Sitting in the warm car, almost home at their farm, she was thinking about Hans. How was his Christmas that year? She imagined him giving his "Kamaraden" an American cigarette each and feeling warm in his heart. She was sure that he did not forget that Christmas tree either. She knew that Hans, her first love, left the next March, the only surviving son of a widow, to join his "Mutti" in Germany. She wondered if he was possibly still alive and maybe, just maybe, thinking about the same Christmas tree as she was at this moment. After all, it was just four days before Christmas.

****

The car stopped. It was now dark. The darkness falls early in northern Alberta in winter. Their dog, Blackberry, came to welcome them, and the husband asked if she would like him to make supper—potato pancakes. He knew she loved them, and he loved them even more. So she happily agreed.

The woman understood why her man refused to mess up the car with the beautiful tree. Although he was far from being a freak about order, he loved his car clean, neat and empty. Emphasis was on empty.

But she was constantly filling the car with objects: letters to politicians and Christian prisoners, baking for grandkids and friends, boxes of used clothing for this or that mom or the thrift store, books for the library, pails of scraps and leftovers for her elderly—very elderly—hens, shredded paper to provide bedding for them, empty egg cartons, and so on.

Good man as he was, he considered all this activity very commendable. He just wished his wife somehow accomplished them all without using the car. Perhaps a flying carpet would do. But although she hooked quite a few carpets in her life, so far she had not manage to hook one with such a capacity.

Presently, as he was peeling potatoes, she was picking up some of his socks from the floor, his newspapers from the kitchen table and pens he used last evening. After this general tidying, she realized that today, after a long time, they had traveled home from Grande Prairie empty: no pails, no boxes, no nothing. Perhaps it was his Christmas wish to have the car clean and empty, and that wish came true.

Why He Decorates the Tree

SHE TURNED ON THE CHRISTMAS TREE LIGHTS. THE TREE HAD been cut and decorated by her husband a few days before.

For long years it was the woman and the children, while they were home, who would decorate the tree. Almost every year the kids would make some new ornaments, and after they got their driver's licenses they would be the ones who drove to a nearby spruce forest and cut the Christmas trees. Then they would decorate them with her participation with paper ornaments, embroidered ornaments, unelegant paper chains, and also the wonderful Christmas glittery balls of all colours.

Then one Christmas came when she was profoundly unhappy. She refused to have any Christmas tree. The adult children were not coming home for Christmas. She did not see why they should have a tree. All she could remember about Christmas was darkness and pain. Her grandpa died on Christmas. Her uncle died on Christmas. Her mother died on Christmas. Her mother-in-law died on Christmas. Christmases

13

were filled with a stupid fat red dwarf called Claus. Christmas was becoming Xmas. The local school had a pink Barbie concert instead of a Christmas concert, because one dad said he wanted no carols about Jesus at school. "No religion, please. If I want religion, I'll go to church," he sneered. The rest of the parents did not care. Christians did not care. Pastors did not care.

Neither could she remember anybody ever thanking her for "doing Christmas," for baking Christmas cookies and Christmas bread, for cleaning and cooking, for making Christmas gifts or buying gifts with the little money she had for them, for packing gifts or for sending cards. Why should she care to do it?

That year her mailbox was filled with pictures of families—not the Holy Family, mind you—or cards covered with bunnies, puppies or cats and filled with news about the senders and their babies. There was nothing about Baby Jesus.

Also, her personal problems and insecurities made her very, very unhappy and too weak to rally her will for defence. She desired only to lie down, weep and sleep.

She told her husband she refused to have a tree, to bake, to cook, to clean. She was very, very unhappy and unable to pretend, as mothers and wives often do, that everything was okay.

Being a man of few words, unless the subject was politics or religion, he said in one short sentence that he would take care of the Christmas tree.

His greatest weakness was that he was absolutely unable to ever console anybody with words or hugs. Maybe he did not realize it, but the woman did, and it was making her life very lonely. But he went to the forest to cut a small tree. He decorated it with Christmas lights, with all the old paper decorations his little children had made in past years, with decorations embroidered by his daughters and with inelegant handmade paper chains. She observed him as he quietly worked on it with his unsteady hands and realized that he, too, was sad. And it dawned on her that he was sad because she was not well, and he was doing it all for her because he loved her and wanted to bring some cheer into her heart but was unable to do it with words and hugs.

The woman appreciated that from that Christmas on the man always took care of their Christmas trees, choosing them and cutting them in the forest, decorating them and taking them down after Epiphany, the feast of the Three Kings. Every year, when he proceeded with his custom, when he picked a handsaw and left on foot for the forest to get the tree, she remembered how the first time he took on this responsibility it had consoled her and filled her with peace and reassurance of his love.

An Earlier Healing Christmas Tree

HIS LOVING ACTION BROUGHT TO HER MIND A CLEAR enlightening remembrance of a similar situation many years before, a memory of the Christmas in her homeland the year her sister died, of a Christmas tree she had forgotten about but now came with fullness back to her mind and heart. It was a Christmastime when she brought similar consolation to her mom, so these two special Christmas trees became bound together in her heart with a strange clarity. They belonged together. The first tree happened to help her to see the second one in its true Christmas light. Maybe she would never have realized the Christmas light of the second tree if not for the first one.

That light also came without words or hugs, for she was a mere child at the time, and it was her mother who was weeping, weak, unhappy, unwilling to have a Christmas tree and denying herself any happiness after her dear child died so unexpectedly.

17

It was also four days before Christmas many years ago, and the girl realized Mom still had not bought a Christmas tree. Mom had looked sick and tired for a long time, but that day she was exceptionally pale. Her eyes were red. She was moving with difficulty.

The woman now knew what she did not know then, that her mom was going through a deep depression.

After returning from her manual job in the brick factory and starting to cook and clean, Mom interrupted the heavy silence. She turned to her daughter, who had asked about the tree, and promised to buy a tree the next day. But the days went by, and it came to the last day before Christmas Eve day, the day of the traditional Czech Christmas celebration. Last day of school. No tree!

"We will not have a Christmas tree this year," the mother told her daughter in an exhausted voice. "Your sister died. I have no strength to go to the city for a tree. What is there to celebrate? Your sister is dead! I'll just put the gifts on the table in our bedroom."

Even now the woman does not know what made her say, "Mom, I'll go to the city for a tree." It was some movement in her heart, undeciphered, unclear.

"You would go? There might be none left…"

"I'll go."

So Mom gave her some money for the tree and some for the streetcar.

Never before had the girl gone shopping alone in the city. She did not know where one could buy a tree, but something positive in her was assuring her that she'd manage.

Arriving in the centre of Ostrava, she realized it was almost dark. Stores would soon close their doors. She knew she had to hurry.

At once she spotted a man with a Christmas tree waiting for the street tram. "Sir, please, where did you buy the tree? My mom has sent me to buy one, but I don't know where to go."

The man showed surprise on his face because it was very unusual in those times and places to be addressed by strangers. The girl knew that it was not proper, but she had to get a Christmas tree! In her eagerness to get help from him, she told him all. She told him about her sister, about the sad mother who did not want to have a Christmas tree. The chagrin of her heart flew out of her to the darkened street and left her lightened.

The man's face changed as he listened with sympathy. He replied with a soft, kind voice and explained how to get to a small square, Kuri Rynek—the Chicken Square. He warned her that only a few trees were left there so she should hurry, and she did, consoled by his kindness.

Almost nobody was walking in the streets. The streetlamps were poor, but she was glad for them. She found the square in no time, arriving just as the seller was about to throw the last five trees into the big garbage bin. His nose was red. While it was not freezing, it was not pleasant to stand outside the whole day without any shelter. He wanted to go home.

The girl's heart rejoiced. She assessed all the trees left in the yard. All symmetry seemed to avoid them. They had poor branches. But she did not mind. She took hold of one, hugged it as though it was her sister, paid three crowns to the man, and with true joy hurried to the tram station. For the first time in her life, she was carrying a Christmas tree. This one was small and light.

The streetcar was empty. The conductor sold her a ticket for the ride, and because happiness is contagious, seeing her happy face he smiled at her. Christmas was coming after all!

After the half-hour ride, she still had a kilometre to walk through dark, empty streets. There was no snow, and dry leaves from the park were blown under her feet. Stars were shining. The girl was at peace. She was not looking forward to getting nice Christmas gifts under her tree. Usually there were just practical things for them, plus, perhaps, a book. But she felt great. For her, Christmas had just arrived!

She felt that to have Christmas was a natural thing, that there should always be a Christmas once a year, and that there should be a Christmas tree to mark the Christmas. She felt as if the planet Earth was commanded by some eternal verdict to celebrate Christmases. She felt that this very law spoke to her and made her do what she did, and she felt that it was a good, precious, heart-filling law. Because she obeyed it, she was content.

After supper, with the help of her brother, she put the decorations on the Christmas tree. It was a cherished tree. Its glitter brought normalcy, peace and quiet joy. Near the top of the tree, a paper pig of faded gold was placed, as on every Christmas, to remind all of the duration of love. Mom relaxed, looked peaceful, and seemed to have more strength.

Next evening there was fish soup, fried carp, potato salad, yummy poppy seed cake and some Christmas cookies. The braided Christmas bread was presiding on the table.

Last Christmas her very artistic, now deceased, sister decorated the bread with a snippet from the Christmas tree and a bow. She also pinned snippets on the white damask tablecloth. She certainly had had a talent for making things beautiful!

The girl made the same arrangement in memory of her sister, and it, too, was beautiful.

The whole family gathered for the Christmas Eve supper: Grandma Anna and Grandpa Francis, Aunt Alice and Uncle

Ludwig, half-sister Dana and her husband. Only one chair was empty, one set of plates not filled during the evening, as was the Christian Christmas custom of their region. The place and plate were for the one who died last year.

But there was peace and no more tears.

It was Christmas.

Potato Pancakes

THE MAN INVITED HIS WIFE TO THE TABLE. THE GOLDEN, crunchy pancakes, the very masterpiece of his culinary talents, were ready. The smell was promising, and, after a short prayer, she started to eat. Fried potato pancakes must be eaten fresh and hot. The man served his wife first, and only after she had her share did he fry some for his own plate.

They were silent. He was silent because he was a man of few words. She was silent because she knew it was not easy to engage him in conversation, unless the topics were politics or religion, and she didn't feel like either.

So she kept to herself, thinking about potato pancakes.

Jewish people call them "latkes" and traditionally fry them when they celebrate Hanukah. It couldn't be an original Jewish meal, because the land of Israel did not have potatoes during the time of the first Hanukah. It must have been the Ashkenazy Jews, who lived in Europe for many years, who "invented" latkes soon after potatoes landed in the fields of poor people, for all Europeans know, make and love potato pancakes. So potato pancakes became a traditional Jewish Hanukah meal, fried in oil in memory of the sacred oil that lasted in their temple for many days during the great oil shortage at the time of the first Hanukah.

The woman also loved potatoes, considering them a true gift from God. Washing dishes after the meal, she started to sing to herself a cute Russian song about potatoes. She had learned it in school, and it made her think about her childhood and later about her children.

Her husband was resting on the couch, reading the *National Post*. Many bad things had happened during the last few days, and he wanted to know all about them.

The Crèche

So the woman went to the tree to caress it with her eyes, hands and heart—the lights, the paper ornaments, the embroidered ornaments, the inelegant paper chains that little hands had worked on so diligently many years ago.

A very primitive nativity scene was standing under the tree, and she lifted it to touch it with her hands and to feel the love still flowing out of it. It was constructed from an old wooden mandarin orange box and filled with figurines painted on sturdy cardboard with some basic, now faded, colours. The beautiful sheep of the manger looked like wolves, the cattle's legs were crumbling from age, and Mary was portrayed with the fervour of a Cubist. The roof was crafted from the same brown cardboard, covered with cut paper pretending to be straw, with each straw lovingly and individually glued to the roof.

Presently, above the roof between the Christmas lights, she caught the happy little starry eyes of her tiny son floating on the blue and silvery mist of the air, and another Christmas tree of the past presented itself to her mind.

It happened many years before, while they were living in Quebec. She was pregnant with their last child and very unhappy. She was not yet aware that one can influence one's feelings to a great degree, so she was not even trying to be happy. The emigration was very difficult for her. Deprived of language, family and friends, she felt so lonely!

She returned from the doctor's office that day just in time to make lunch for their daughter and son, who walked daily to school, then home for lunch, back to school and home again. While she was serving the soup and sandwiches, the phone rang.

It was her husband, asking how was she and what the doctor had said. She told him the doctor had informed her that in Canada husbands were welcomed in the hospital during deliveries. She begged her husband to come with her when the time came. She feared hospitals. She had given birth to their two children in Communist hospitals. There she went through a very intimidating, painful experience, and lonely, so lonely! One suffered and fought alone.

Her husband was taken off guard. No, he would not go. "Birthing is a female affair. Men go at that time to the pub to pre-celebrate. Whoever came up with this modernity? It is not 'manly' to be present at the delivery." He tried to joke about it.

Her voice faltered and she started to cry. Her husband had to return to his desk. So she was crying loudly with all the despair of her soul. Loud, very loud, covering her face and leaning on a wall.

Somebody hugged her legs. A little voice spoke. Her little son said, "Maminko, I will go with you to the hospital to help you give birth to the baby." His eyes filled with concern, with pain.

She burst into laughter, the laughter of joy, encouraged by his love and his courage. It made her instantly strong!

The snow came early that November, and the man promised their son to build a crèche with him. They brought moss from the forest, and the boy was unable to keep the secret. He told his mom he would make a manger with Dad for her, to make her happy.

Soon a baby girl was born, and the man went with her to the hospital after all. She did not ask him again, but he went with her anyway. He helped her to breathe, counted the seconds between contractions, witnessed the pain.

The doctor, who was also the mayor of the town, came late from a council meeting, slightly intoxicated, just in time to catch the baby girl, turning her elegantly and swiftly to make her gasp for breath and make herself heard. A few minutes later he smoked a cigarette with the happy father.

The Canadian hospital experience was much different! There was no intimidation, no male cleaning service with mops and pails during her delivery as in Czechoslovakia. Her husband was with her, stunned by the process but faithfully staying with her. No words, no hugs, but he would squeeze her hand, and she felt his love.

Christmas was coming fast. Soon it was clear to their son that Dad had abandoned the project of building the manger. Dad never was a handyman.

To make his mom happy, the boy started on the project alone, closing the door of his room to do his "homework." The child gathered the material and, without any help, crafted the crèche. How proud he was of it! When he presented it to her, she cried, just like now. His eyes—the little stars.

Under the Christmas tree that year, a fluffy orange Snoopy was found for the new sister. The woman knew it cost the children all the quarters they were getting from her occasionally to buy some sweets. Snoopy was a gift of sacrifice and love for the little baby, and he never left her side until a handsome tall young man pushed him out of her bed. Even now, his body patched and repaired many times, Snoopy was still treasured and loved by her, kept in a secret place so her kids would not damage him more.

The Christmas tree with the Christmas crèche and with an orange Snoopy now floated out of the woman's mind because her husband spoke to her. "I'll go watch Fox News now." The woman went with him, but before she left she turned off the Christmas tree lights and thought again of the beautiful tree with the golden sash and a sign, "Free for taking." She wondered if it was still standing by the bus stop and the pink school in Grande Prairie or if the good Lord had already led to it the person for whom it was predestined.

Taking Christ Out of Christmas

THERE WAS A SIGNIFICANT PORTION OF BAD NEWS ON FOX. Christmas trees were disappearing from stores and city squares, and clerks in stores were forbidden to wish customers "Merry Christmas" because some people wanted to spoil the joy of Christmas for everybody. They complained that Christmas was a religious holiday and should not be mentioned to them because they were of a different religion, and it greatly upset them to hear the word "Christ" in "Christmas." The woman wondered if the same people also refused their holiday pay because it originated in Christ and His birth. She knew the answer: no, they took it all. They took the paid holiday gladly, and if approached about it, they would for sure say, "It is just a statutory holiday!" So even they partook somehow of Christ's gifts. The gift of Himself continued even to those who hated Him—in a nice Christmas paid holiday package.

It also came to her that, with some exceptions, nobody ever refused to come to a child's or neighbour's or friend's birthday party. Neither did they object to celebrating Queen Victoria's birthday with fireworks, picnics, sports, cakes.

But the birthday of the King of kings, the birthday of the King of the universe, they didn't want to celebrate. How sad!

She left *Fox News* in need of cheer. All this was so much like her Communist childhood. God was pushed out of Czechoslovakian society in the name of atheism, science and progress. Now in Canada and the U.S.A., He was being pushed out in the name of tolerance, multiculturalism and "being nice to others." But the goal was the same. Soon Canada might turn into Narnia under the White Witch, a cold and white country where it was always winter and never Christmas.

First Christmas in Canada

FOR HERSELF, SHE HAD MADE A DECISION A LONG TIME AGO. SHE would always celebrate Christ's birth. So she went back to her kitchen. It was time to take out more Christmas decorations. She pulled several tablecloths out of a drawer. They were small, some with hand embroidered candles and Christmas greenery, others with cones, stars and bells. All were white and starched, breathing festivity into the air. At last she pulled out one that was big, greyish, tattered, with no Christmas theme. She kissed it and thanked God for Mr. and Mrs. Dussault, the French Canadian couple who received them into their home after they first came to Canada and cared for them. Because the Dussaults were planning to sell their small cottage, they gave the immigrants lots of useful things that were no longer needed. The woman remembered how shy she was, almost ashamed to take anything from the table of offered things. But the kind Madame encouraged her again and again to take the pots, pans, cups, plates, an old kitchen mixer and a tablecloth.

She remembered reaching first for the tablecloth, because in her country and family a tablecloth was always an inviting symbol of friendship, order and meals. There had always been tablecloths on her tables, but not now. She came as a refugee with nothing but $50, a husband and two small children.

It was four days to Christmas. Now she was given a tablecloth, and her husband later found a yard where Scouts were selling trees. He purchased one, fresh from the forest, not too big, not too full, but beautiful.

The price was very high, and he had not expected it. It represented their food bill for three days. Now nothing was left for even tiny plastic toys for the children. No Christmas gifts for his kids. He was mad.

Whenever he got mad, it made the woman very unhappy, but she had agreed to emigrate with him to Canada, to flee the Communist oppression after the Russian armies occupied Czechoslovakia in 1968, so she kept back her tears. She knew fish was cheap at that time, and she had already baked a plate of cookies, planning on having at least the traditional Christmas Eve supper, even if not gifts.

But the Lord is good! While she did not care much about Him at that time, He did care for her. The Dussault family invited them for la veille de Noël, their Christmas Eve celebration. Their numerous family members were all present. Each of them brought a Christmas gift for the refugee children. Never before or after did they get so many presents: colouring books, crayons, watercolours, small toys, chocolates, a dominoes game...

Neither the woman nor the children understood any of the gay conversation. Only her husband did. He loved to learn new languages and had taught himself some French while still in Czechoslovakia.

The woman was lonely, thinking about her mother and father, about the new furniture and garden she left behind, her friends and planned studies at the university. It was all gone, which made her very sad. But she was also thankful, thankful for all these good Catholic people who made her children so happy, who made their Christmas.

Back in their apartment the children placed the gifts on the only table there was. The table was covered with a tablecloth, and on it stood a Christmas tree sparingly decorated with paper snowflakes, paper birds in paper cages and paper butterflies. There was also a small flask of gin, sent by her brother from Czechoslovakia. She did not know how it made it to their table, because at that time the Canadian postal service was refusing to deliver any alcohol. Well, miracles happen, and it was Christmas.

The tablecloth was used heavily for three years. Later her mother sent some new ones by mail. So this one became a memorial tablecloth, to be used only at Christmas in memory of that first Canadian Christmas. Every time it was pulled out, she would remember her fears and anxieties, the difficult first years, and was thankful to God for His people, who are His hands on earth.

She laid it now on the kitchen table, touching tenderly the faded pictures of watering cans, cacti and flowers, remembering the unexpected gifts under that one tree of Christmas past and the joy of their children, and hoping that somehow the Lord would lift her present feelings of thanks and bring them to the original owners of the tablecloth, who by this time were with Him.

Nighttime on the Farm

THE WOMAN CUDDLED THEIR DOG, WHO NOW FOR MANY YEARS did not sleep outside but inside the house. She hoped the coyotes would not come near at night. The old dog, Blackberry, still kept her role of a guardian, and at least once, sometimes three times, in a night started to bark violently, sniffing or hearing some enemies outside, waking the woman and demanding to be let out. In spite of her arthritis, Blackberry would shoot out of the door and make a ruckus under the stars. Sometimes she would chase the enemies for ten minutes, sometimes for thirty. She would return afterwards and scratch at the door violently, now demanding to be let in. While the woman was thankful for the guardian services, we must say that for several years now she had not had a good night's sleep.

During many powerful scratching exercises, the dog drilled a hole through the door. The woman's brother, Karel, put in a not-so-new free-for-taking door he found somewhere. The not-so-new door was now without ventilation, and the woman, who did not like drafts, protected the door from further paw drilling with a big piece of sturdy blue plastic, also donated by her brother. She had attached it to the door with a silvery frame of duct tape. It looked awful. However, by now she had learned to live with less-than-perfect things, creatures and self. She had learned during her life that we must bear many imperfections with love.

She still loved all that was beautiful and perfect, so now she looked out of the window, where perfection was always to be found—the black sky with millions of stars, the northern perfect beauty! Just last November, when her grandkids were at the farm, the little boys, Gideon and Reuben, had exclaimed with great excitement, "Babi, you have so many stars here. Millions! It's beautiful. We in Edmonton don't have many stars. Awesome!" (*Babi* means "Granny" in Czech.)

"Yes, the Lord gave them to me," she bragged. "He gave them to me to look upon and learn how to count in millions. In the city you have millions of lights on the ground, so you cannot see the heavenly lights. That's why I live on a farm, to see what is not to be seen in the city."

The stars were silent, yet alive. She was unable to explain it, but it felt like a humungous, beautiful, living world.

Her husband came to kiss her good night, and she made a small sign of the cross, as was her custom (and her mother's custom, and her grandmother's custom before her), on his forehead and blessed him with a prayer for protection. He swallowed some pills, she swallowed her one pill, and to bed they went. His was in his office room, where he could watch TV in bed into the night. The woman disliked most TV entertainment, so she slept in their bedroom. She read her Bible, then closed her eyes, but as she was falling asleep the enemies of her rest started a pack fight not far away from the farmhouse, and Blackberry had to go out to scare them off. So out of her warm bed the woman climbed and into the cold night Blackberry disappeared.

Resting back on her pillow, the woman decided to wait for the dog's return. There is nothing so unpleasant as to be awakened from a smooth dive into dreamland! She again remembered the beautiful tree, "Free for taking," standing a night watch outside the pink school. Was it still there under the northern stars, waiting for its destiny?

The Christmas Tree Forest

ANOTHER CHRISTMAS TREE CAME TO HER MIND. THIS ONE WAS also a tree of many Christmases past and belonged to her little niece. It was a French-speaking Christmas tree in Montreal.

Her niece was not of school age yet. She was a born leader, creative, imaginative, inventive, and lived in a complex of apartment houses with other not-so-well-off families and children. In those days, kids often played in front of their homes most of the day. Without cable TV or computers, they had to find their own entertainment and friends. Also, fear for their safety was not so great in those days.

The little girl loved the outdoors, camping and forests; she preferred them to the city scene. She loved her Christmas tree and was very disappointed when the time came to part with it. Deprived of its ornaments and lights, the tree was lying on a heap of many discarded Christmas trees by a garbage bin, waiting to be collected on Friday for burning in some garbage dump.

As she jumped off the two house steps into a fresh, mild winter day, her big blue eyes filled with tears for the trees. A few of her friends were outside too, screaming at her to join them in a game. "No, not today. You know what? Let's build a forest!" she screamed back, hit by a splendid inspiration.

An hour later she rushed home to ask her mom for dry mittens. Hers were totally wet. She was so excited, so loud! "Mom, we're building a forest! Tonight we could pull out our tent and we could camp there! Great! Awesome! Soon squirrels and bunnies will move into our forest. It will be very beautiful! Oh, Mom!"

Whatever, thought her mom silently. All moms of the world have such reactions many times daily, but to her daughter she replied, "Wonderful, love!" happy that her little girl was somehow occupied outside, because she was busy sewing a dress for her child.

After another hour the little girl insisted with all joy and might that Mom had to go with her for a walk in the forest. So Mom put on a coat and warm hat, abandoned her sewing, and out she walked with her daughter. Behold, there before her eyes was a forest! Her daughter commanded such inspiration in her friends that, in a chain reaction, her inspiration was passed on to more children. All the discarded Christmas trees from near and far were pulled together to make a forest.

In those days, people cherished real trees, and city bylaws had not outlawed them yet, so very few trees were artificial. Close to two hundred trees had been salvaged from the tall apartment buildings by some twenty preschoolers and planted firmly in the snow wherever it was piled high enough to hold a Christmas tree. Some stuffed teddy bears and bunnies were already inhabiting the charming woods of the children's fantasy. Twenty proud, happy little foresters were busy making trails, planning log cottages, cardboard houses and camping places!

The first time the woman heard this story, her heart melted in a prayer. "God Almighty, please help me see the world again through a child's eyes." In reality, for many years she would wear black glasses. Now she knew how wrong it was.

There was lots of crying when the garbage collectors came to pick up without mercy the discarded Christmas trees—the beautiful dream of the children's hearts. The collectors were grouchy because they had to pick up the trees individually, which took lots of time. They were paid to clean the city, not embellish it!

The dog returned and scratched at the blue plastic. The woman let her in, thanked her for guarding and begged her to sleep tight. Back in her bed, she sent a prayer to God. "Please help me to see how I can take old things, experiences, forgotten friends and unwanted people, and make something new from it, bring some dream into life! Help me to be a builder, not a destroyer, please!"

She imagined her niece's Christmas tree forest planted around garbage bins in dreary city back lanes with well hugged teddies and bunnies. At once a beautiful spruce tree with a golden sash and a sign, "Free for taking," appeared among them.

How much do we possess, how much does God give us daily, "Free for taking" through our eyes, ears, hearts? How much do we also have to give free? But we ignore most of the gifts and are unwilling to give ourselves.

Christmas Eve Now

THE GREAT DAY ARRIVED. SOON AFTER LUNCH THE WOMAN started to fill the clean, empty car with plates of breaded fish not yet cooked, a pot of fish soup, several loaves of braided Christmas bread and several empty washed pails for chicken food. She added some *National Post*s that their daughter had shared with her dad, now to be shared with his brother-in-law. There were letters to be mailed, a box of Christmas cookies, two gifts for her husband, plus two gifts for her from him. Soon the car was full again. It was no flying carpet, just a well-filled white car. "Pity, pity my dear man," sighed the woman.

First they had to stop to pick up mail. There were some cards with family pictures and news about the families. The woman rejoiced at the good news, was sad about the sad news. She gladly opened cards with true Christmas pictures. Only one red dwarf was stuck forever in a tight chimney. A Hanukah card combined with a Merry Christmas wish was there too.

The woman was happy and started to sing some Christmas carols. The country was flying by, with snowy fields, crooked trees in the ditches and big black birds. Soon they reached Grande Prairie.

In the city, they went first to visit her brother and his wife, to see their Christmas tree. It was a forest tree, very natural, with electric lights and also real red and white candles. Near the treetop was a hundred-year-old golden paper pig.

"May you stay there forever," wished the woman. She touched the pig for all the love that ever went into Christmases, for all the love of God the Father and His Son, who came to earth as our greatest gift, for all the love for little boys and girls that ever goes into each Christmas, and for their happiness as they learn about the joy of gifts and giving. From there the path leads humans to experience and learn the joy of life, the joy of faith and the joy of hope for a God-filled eternity.

Her brother, Karel, was decorating a big bowl of his excellent potato salad for the supper, almost ready for the big celebration.

From there they drove to their daughter's place, and the woman could hardly wait to pass by the pink school. Of course, the "Free for taking" tree with the golden sash was gone, and she rejoiced. She naturally told all their children and grandkids about the tree and of her joy, but they paid little attention. The little ones were too excited, and the big ones were too busy. Nevertheless, soon they all went to church, and after the worship service they settled down to the festive supper: fish soup with croutons, great potato salad, fried fish, Christmas bread and cookies, and special cheeses.

To amuse the little children, the woman told them about an old legend of animals speaking in human tongues at midnight on Christmas Eve. The legend says that because Christmas Eve is a very special night when Christ was born and the whole creation expected his birth, animals were given special powers to rejoice with angels and humans. Now again the whole creation expects His return, and in memory and hope of His coming the animals again receive the ability to converse in human languages at midnight each Christmas Eve. The tiny kids listened with open mouths and believed the legend. The bigger kids loved the story, disbelieved it, but kept silent.

After supper, the adults sang an ancient Czech carol, Narodil se Christus Pan—Lord Christ Was Born—and most of them and all of the children were commanded to retire into one room, in expectation of the Baby Jesus or His angels coming with gifts. They had to keep absolutely silent to hear the tinkling of their Christmas bells. It took a long time for the angels to come and unload the gifts. Finally the bell was heard, and the stampede of tiny feet sounded through the whole house. Down the stairs they ran, and they exclaimed with joy and laughter, "Wow! So many gifts!"

The tree was splendid, very thick, almost without scent, glittering, and its lower branches were outstretched like open hands, offering piles of gifts on the floor around it. The children were ecstatic. The woman was not too happy. She did not like opulence, but since her children were very generous and always shared lots with others, she did not know what to think or if she had the right to be unhappy. The little grandkids were very happy, so she decided to be happy for them and thank God for His blessings. Did she know what the future held for the children? Maybe one day they might not have even a Christmas tree, just memories. Shouldn't they be happy memories?

Some general cleaning was done after the gifts were opened and shared, and all helped. The adults were sipping wine or some special Scotch, and the children were playing, happy and tired. Some adults were preparing to go to midnight mass.

On the Farm the Night Before Christmas

THE WOMAN AND HER HUSBAND WERE GETTING READY TO GO back to the farm. The little three, Gideon, Reuben and Trinity, wanted her to stay and tell them some "good night stories," but the woman said, "No way. I want once and forever to find out if the legend of talking animals is true or false. I have to be home at the farm at midnight to spy on our kittens and the dog.

"Tomorrow we will come back for Christmas dinner of turkey, cranberry sauce and mashed potatoes. So by then I'll know and tell you all about it," she promised, and it consoled them.

The woman was rather tired, and her husband also, because he was in a way the chef of the festive Christmas Eve feast. Through the dark night they were driving. Almost no vehicles stood in their way, so the man was not tempted to pass anybody and went rather slow. The woman looked for the Northern Lights, but for several years they had been almost nonexistent. The radio played classical Christmas music and hymns. The

47

woman hoped to go to bed before midnight but at once remembered her promise. Well, I must reveal that when she was promising to stay awake until midnight, she did not take her own promise too seriously. She did not really believe that the old legend might be true.

Maybe on the very night of Christ's birth in Bethlehem, when cosmic angels were present to witness, announce and protect the divine birth, when the big star appeared, when shepherds and their sheep came to see the Baby Messiah, maybe on that night animals spoke in human tongues. The Bible does not tell us so, but the Bible does tell us a true story of a donkey speaking to a prophet, a long time ago, to warn him of God's wrath. Such miracles can happen on very, very special occasions, but not now, not today. But she promised, right?

"Oh well," said the woman to herself. "I'll put on the tree lights, bring the kitties and the dog inside. I'll talk to them, pet them, hug them. It is Christmas, and I've had no time to cuddle them yet. I'll go to bed after midnight."

She did as she promised. Both kittens, Mikesh and Jakesh (pronounced Meekesh and Yakesh), were delighted to be inside with the humans and the dog. At first they played with the dog's tail, but the dog did not like it. Then they started jumping from the couch onto the kitchen table. The very special Christmas tablecloth would slide with them, and they enjoyed it greatly. It was a great sport of kitten skating!

The woman reprimanded them nicely for their behaviour, but they couldn't care less. Afraid for her tablecloth, she folded it, and the jumps onto the table lost their sliding effect. To avoid boredom, the kittens were wrestling for some time until shortly before midnight. Jakesh discovered that she could hit the red and silvery Christmas ornaments on the tree and the ornaments would swing and swing. Wow, what fun!

48

The woman was not amused, and when the kitten decided to climb the Christmas tree, she had had enough. It was just past midnight, her animals did not speak in a human tongue, of course, and she did not expect them to, as I said.

After the woman yelled at Jakesh, her husband grabbed the kitty to save the tree and to throw the cat outside. This was just too much! As he was carrying the furry ball and opening the door, the kitten screamed very loud in a human voice, "Ne, ne!" (pronounce neh, neh). The woman jumped up, and her husband dropped the kitty in surprise. In their mother Czech language, "ne, ne" means "no, no!" Jakesh darted into the night.

The woman was amazed, realizing only later that she missed the opportunity of her life to have a Czech conversation with a kitty cat. She went to bed not believing herself, but there was a witness, her husband. The kitty spoke in a human tongue, in Czech!

In her bed, she was tossing, tired but unable to sleep. Again and again she would see behind her closed eyes Jakesh hitting the tree ornaments, trying to climb the tree, her husband grabbing her, opening the door, and the clear human screaming in the Czech language, "No, no!" Jakesh seemingly did not want to leave the amusement park the house was offering to her. "Why did I not call her back?" wondered the woman. "What a story I have to tell everybody tomorrow! They will not believe me!"

Christmas Day

BUT THEY DID! SHE HAD A WITNESS. THE ADULTS CONSIDERED it a very charming story and no doubt were thinking of some natural explanation for the rare scream. Perhaps the man pushed somehow on the kitty's lungs carrying her out, and it produced sounds resembling human words. The older children were tempted, oh so very tempted, to believe in talking animals, but stopped short of it. The enchanted youngest ones believed it all and got excited. Their eyes were shining.

Little Reuben told his parents that he would not sleep in his aunt's house because he wanted to go to Grandma's and Grandpa's farm to talk to the animals. His older brother cooled his resolve. "Silly, the animals can speak in human tongues only between midnight Christmas Eve and Christmas Day morning. We have to be there at that time, when the miracle happens. It's all over now. We'll go to the farm tomorrow, and you will not hear them speak human anymore."

"Maybe next Christmas you could spend at our farm," the woman consoled Reuben. "Maybe they will speak once again in human tongues." To tell the truth, she did not believe it could happen again, while she did not doubt it did happen and it was a miracle.

Miracles happen on purpose. God is in all miracles.

Perhaps He did not want her to forget one more Christmas tree, the one with a golden sash and the sign "Free for taking," which the kind stranger helped her to bring to the pink school and the bus stop.

Why was she inspired to tell her family the ancient legend, really a silly story? Who knew her husband would grab a kitten later at night in such a way that its scream would sound like a human voice crying in Czech, "No, no!"? Didn't her grandkids have a faith, a faith like a small mustard seed, in animals speaking in human tongues? Wasn't God perhaps reminding her again about the power of faith in Him? Wasn't He perhaps teaching the little grandchildren their first faith lesson? Faith is filled with miracles, and miracles are real. Did He, perhaps, want to make the adults look at Christmas fresh through children's eyes?

After all, wasn't the first Christmas the greatest miracle of all—God's Son coming to the planet Earth to save His creation, the whole creation, humans and everything else, from the curse of disobedience and death?

This, His salvation, is "Free for Taking" to those who would have it, like the tree she tied by the pink school.

Somebody else paid for the tree: their daughter.

Somebody else paid for the earth's salvation: Jesus, the Son of God, the Lamb of God.

Oh Christmas tree, oh Christmas tree, you stand in verdant beauty.

THE END

About the Author

ASTRID WAS BORN IN THE TROUBLED YEARS OF WORLD WAR II in what is today the Czech Republic. It was then the German-occupied Protectorate of Bohemia and Moravia. Times were dangerous and sad, filled with terror. The little joy she got in those years was given to her by her Grandma Anna. Anna would tell Astrid and her sister stories of happy days and of her own childhood. So Astrid always identified happiness and joy with stories, books, and theatre. In them she flew away from anxious reality.

Soon after the war ended, a Communist dictatorship took over in Czechoslovakia, and the times continued to be full of fear. Astrid took one year of college education to work in a library or a bookstore. Soon she was working in a bookstore and reading hundreds of books. She also worked part-time as a director of a small children's theatre and wrote and directed several children's plays.

In 1968 Czechoslovakia tried to bring in democracy, but the Prague Spring was suppressed by the armies of the Warsaw Pact. By God's mercy Astrid and her husband, Ivo, were able to escape and emigrate to Canada with their two children.

Emigration was extremely difficult for her, and in real despair she remembered what her mother taught her, that there is a God, the God of love, and He has a son, Jesus Christ. Her conversion was miraculous, and with the help of local Baptist pastor Murray Heron she learned with joy about God and His Son.

Astrid helped her husband with his translation of C. S. Lewis's book *The Problem of Pain.* This book was published and smuggled to Czechoslovakia by the Catholic Academy in Rome. She then, with the help of her husband, translated *The Pilgrim's Regress* from the same author, but before Rome published it, Communism in her homeland collapsed. So the book, as well as her Czech children's storybook *The One Who Never Sleeps*, was published in Czechoslovakia.

An avid pro-lifer, Astrid wrote and directed two pro-life plays, *Is It So?* and *The Seed.* She occasionally writes for some Czech pro-life and conservative periodicals. She is involved in Christian politics and helping the persecuted Church.

For some years Astrid was employed part-time by her husband, Ivo, a professional engineer. Thanks to his support she was able to pursue her writing, volunteering, and artwork. He loves the illustrations she created for this book and is her faithful driver and helper.

Her brother, Karel Weniger, also helps in her endeavours, like putting on plays and exhibits of Czech art.

Astrid and Ivo are retired and live on a quarter section of land, mostly bush, in Rio Grande, near Beaverlodge, Alberta. They have three children—Dr. Alexandra Noga, Dr. Tom Noga and Anna Noga, PhD of biochemistry—and eight wonderful grandchildren. Their days at the farm are shared with their old dog, Blackberry, cats Jakesh and Mikesh, and a dozen elderly hens.

The Lord is good to them.

CPSIA information can be obtained at www.ICGtesting.com
Printed in the USA
LVOW01s0725100315

429910LV00005B/5/P